THE LOCH NESS MONSTER MYSTERY

MAUREEN FLEMING & VIRGINIA KING

Illustrated by Chris Johnston

Written by Maureen Fleming and Virginia King
Illustrated by Chris Johnston
Designed by Christine Deering and Peter Shaw

Published by Mimosa Publications Pty Ltd
PO Box 779, Hawthorn 3122, Australia
© 1995 Mimosa Publications Pty Ltd

Literacy 2000 is a Trademark registered in the
United States Patent and Trademark Office.

Distributed in the United States of America by

Rigby
A Division of Reed Elsevier Inc.
500 Coventry Lane
Crystal Lake, IL 60014
800-822-8661

Distributed in Canada by
PRENTICE HALL GINN
1870 Birchmount Road
Scarborough
Ontario M1P 2J7

99 98 97 96
10 9 8 7 6 5 4 3 2
Printed in Hong Kong through Bookbuilders Ltd

ISBN 0 7327 1573 3

CONTENTS

THE LOCH

Loch Ness is a deep, cold, windswept lake in the north of Scotland. The loch sits in an enormous crack in the Earth's surface, formed millions of years ago when two huge land masses slipped sideways. Today it is surrounded by lush green hills, and overlooked by the crumbling ruins of Urquhart Castle.

Loch is a Scottish word meaning **lake** or **inlet**.

Loch Ness is the largest freshwater lake in Great Britain. It is approximately 37 kilometers (23 miles) long, up to 1.6 kilometers (one mile) wide, and up to 230 meters (750 feet) deep.

About 18,000 years ago, Scotland was covered with a thick layer of ice. During this time, a huge glacier carved out the floor of Loch Ness to its present depth. When the ice melted, the sea rose and flooded the whole country. Gradually the sea level dropped again, and Loch Ness became "landlocked" except for a shallow channel at each end.

Loch Ness is long and narrow, with steep rocky sides both above and below the waterline. The water is fresh but very dark and murky, because it contains rotting plant material called **peat**. Many people claim that a mysterious creature lives in hidden caves below the loch's surface. There is certainly room for such a creature; Loch Ness is big enough for a whole family of monsters to live in its inky depths.

THE LEGEND

About 1500 years ago, a holy man named Saint Columba visited a small village on the edge of Loch Ness. According to legend, he asked one of the villagers to swim across the loch and fetch a boat from the other side. But as the man swam, a ferocious-looking monster rose from the water and rushed toward him with its jaws wide open, ready to attack.

Saint Columba shouted across the lake in a booming voice, commanding the monster to stop. Instantly, the strange creature turned and fled, leaving the swimmer safe in the water. This was the first recorded sighting of the legendary Loch Ness monster!

SEEING IS BELIEVING

For hundreds of years, people from towns and villages around the loch have reported exciting encounters with a mysterious creature. Today, the Loch Ness monster is an international celebrity. People come to Scotland from all over the world, hoping to catch a glimpse of Nessie.

This famous photo was taken in 1934, by an English surgeon on vacation in Scotland.

The photo on the facing page was taken in 1977 by Anthony "Doc" Shiels, near Urquhart Castle. Here is how he described what he saw: "Its color was greenish-brown, with a paler underside … it turned away from me and straightened its muscular neck before sinking straight down very smoothly …"

Not every monster spotter has been lucky enough to snap a photograph of Nessie, but many have recorded the details of their strange encounters in writing. Many eyewitnesses have given similar descriptions of the creature's appearance and behavior. They all agree that Nessie is unique – a creature quite unlike any other animal on Earth today.

We sat for a wee while and this crackling seemed to be coming nearer and nearer, and then suddenly this big thing appeared out of the trees and started to move down the beach to the water. I couldn't tell if it had a long neck or a short neck because it was pointing right at us. It had a huge body and it moved like a caterpillar as it came out of the trees. It was the color of an elephant, and it seemed to have rather a shiny skin.

We saw two short, round feet at the front and it lurched to one side and put one foot into the water and then the other one. We didn't wait to see the end of it coming out — we got too big a fright.

When we got home we were all sick and couldn't take our tea. We told our Mom and Dad and we were put to bed with a big dose of castor oil.

Margaret Cameron, 1914.

In 1933, a new road was blasted out of the rock along the northern side of Loch Ness. Local newspapers reported many more monster sightings from this time on. Some people think that the blasting created underwater disturbances, causing the monster to surface from underground caves. Others believe that the road simply allowed more people a good view of the water – and anything that might appear in or on it!

STRANGE SPECTACLE ON LOCH NESS

Loch Ness has for generations been credited with being the home of a fearsome-looking monster, but, somehow or other, this legendary creature has always been regarded as a myth, if not a joke. Now, however, comes the news that the beast has been seen once more, for on Friday of last week, a well-known business man, who lives near Inverness, and his wife (a University graduate), when motoring along the north shore of the loch, were startled to see a tremendous upheaval on the loch, which previously had been as calm as the proverbial millpond. The lady was the first to notice the disturbance, and it was her sudden cries which drew her husband's attention to the water.

There, the creature rolled and plunged for fully a minute, its body resembling that of a whale, and the water cascading and churning like a simmering caldron.

Soon, however, it disappeared in a boiling mass of foam. Both onlookers confessed that there was something uncanny about the whole thing, because, apart from its enormous size, the beast, in taking the final plunge, sent out waves that were big enough to have been caused by a passing steamer. The watchers waited for half an hour in the hope that the monster (if such it was) would come to the surface again; but they had seen the last of it.

The Courier, May 2, 1933

As time went on, eyewitness accounts of monster sightings continued. In 1934, Arthur Grant reported almost hitting a creature with his motorcycle as it crossed the road and headed for the loch. Others reported close encounters, too!

OFFICIAL REPORT FORM

Loch Ness Police Station

The body was very hefty. I distinctly saw two front flippers and there seemed to be two other flippers which were behind and which it used to spring from. The tail was very long and very powerful. As a veterinary student, I can say that I have never seen anything in my life like the animal I saw. It had a head rather like a snake or eel, flat at the top, with a large oval eye, longish neck, and longer tail. The body was much thicker toward the tail than was the front portion. It was black or dark brown and had a skin rather like that of a whale.

SIGNATURE *Arthur Grant*

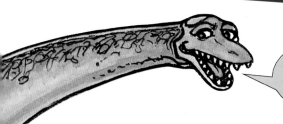

Do you believe these eyewitness reports?

I was out rowing my boat in the middle of the loch, when without any warning, the boat started to heave underneath me. It was terrifying!

My dog was with me in the boat and he leaped from where he was to lie crouching and shivering underneath my seat.

I was really scared. It is the only time I have ever felt frightened on this loch in my whole life.

I can't explain it — the boat just seemed to rise and then stagger back almost immediately.

Believe me. I put my back into the oars to get away from the spot — I didn't even dare move to start the motor!

Alex Campbell. 1955.

In 1982, a Canadian tourist took this photo of the loch. At the time, she didn't notice the strange object breaking the surface of the water. But when the photograph was developed and enlarged …

Is this a monster, or not? What do you think?

ENCOUNTER OF THE NESSIE KIND?

Two visiting American couples believe they had a "hi-tech" encounter with Nessie, it was revealed this week.

The couples were aboard a yacht approaching a point where the depth of Loch Ness reaches 183 meters or 600 feet. Suddenly both of the indicators on their depth reading equipment showed only 1.8 meters or six feet! They immediately cut their engines, thinking they had chanced upon an uncharted mudbank or a shoal of fish. But for some 30 seconds the indicators showed this strange reading. Eventually they returned to their expected reading of 600 feet.

They reported their strange experience to monster hunter Mr. Adrian Shine, who could offer no simple explanation.

Highland News, July 6, 1985

FAMOUS FAKES

But is seeing always believing? In the 1930s, a hunter discovered some enormous footprints on the shore of Loch Ness. Plaster casts were taken of the footprints and sent to the British Museum in London, where scientists concluded that the footprints were fakes.

The hunter had been sent to Loch Ness by a London newspaper keen for a good story. He had made the footprints himself, with the stuffed foot of a hippopotamus that he had brought back from a hunting expedition in Africa!

Photographs of the Loch Ness monster always make news. They keep the mystery alive and attract many tourists to the area.

Photographs can also be sold to newspapers, earning photographers wealth and fame. In 1951, a photographer took a picture that apparently showed the monster's humped back. It convinced some people for many years – until a friend of the photographer revealed that it was really a photo of three bales of hay floating under a tarpaulin!

Have another look at the photograph on page 8. It has been claimed that the monster in the photo is really a toy submarine!

NESSIE THE DINOSAUR?

People who have studied the Loch Ness monster mystery seem to agree that Nessie, if she does exist, looks something like a prehistoric sea creature called a **plesiosaur**. Scientists think plesiosaurs have been extinct for about 70 million years – but they could be wrong. In the early 1900s, a fish called a **coelacanth** was discovered off the coast of East Africa; until then, scientists had believed that the coelacanth had been extinct for almost 60 million years.

What if plesiosaurs survived much longer than scientists believe? One theory is that when Scotland was flooded after the last Ice Age, plesiosaurs swam into Loch Ness from the ocean. Later, when the water level dropped and cut off the loch from the sea, the plesiosaurs might have been trapped inside.

A MONSTER HUNT

Over the years, people have tried many different ways of proving that Nessie exists. The earliest "researchers" dangled weighted lines from rowboats to explore the loch floor. Two adventurous balloonists even tried trailing huge pieces of bacon through the water to lure Nessie to the surface.

NESSIE? WELL, ALMOST!

Dedicated Nessie-hunter Alex Crosbie is convinced he had a near-sighting on Sunday afternoon. Had it not been for the amount of boat traffic on the loch, Nessie would have made an appearance, he claims.

Alex was flying a kite down at Urquhart Castle on Sunday afternoon when he suddenly got the feeling there was something in the water. "There's just something that tells you Nessie is about," he told the *Highland News*.

Alex's method of attracting the shy creature is to throw stones in the water. "It thinks there are fish about," he said. Some of the visitors around the landing stage at Urquhart Castle started to help Alex, and indeed it appeared that there was something jumping around in the water. "I think it was our wee Nessie. But it disappeared."

Undeterred, Alex hopes soon to spend more time on the hunt. To that end he is equipping himself with a zoom lens on his camera. One thing's for sure – Nessie will have to be pretty smart to avoid the attentions of one of her most ardent fans.

Highland News, July 20, 1991

In 1984, a huge monster net was built in a field near the loch and used in an unsuccessful attempt to catch Nessie.

Six years later, a special three-day monster hunt took place on and around Loch Ness. Hundreds of people flocked to the shores of the loch to try their luck. But Nessie kept herself well-hidden, and despite the best efforts of the monster hunters they left empty-handed.

What would you take on a monster hunt?

Perhaps only the development of sophisticated, modern technology would help to reveal the secrets of the loch ...

SCIENCE STEPS IN

Recent scientific expeditions have revealed plenty of new information about the environment and history of Loch Ness, but little about its most famous inhabitant. However, Nessie does have her very own "scientific" name. She was named *Nessiteras Rhombopteryx*, because of some blurry underwater photographs that supposedly show a creature with rhomboid-shaped flippers. Most importantly, having an official name means that Nessie can be protected from harm by British laws designed to ensure the safety of rare animals.

In 1987, a team of scientists and marine biologists known as Operation Deepscan set out to explore the very deepest parts of the loch. In 1992, Project Urquhart – an even more extensive scientific exploration of the loch – was launched.

This scientist is lowering into the loch a remote-controlled submarine with an underwater camera.

Sonar stands for **SO**und **N**avigation **A**nd **R**anging. It is a way of using sound waves to detect the size and location of submerged objects. The sound waves sent out by a ship's sonar system are reflected by objects under the water. Special equipment is used to detect and measure these reflected "echoes," and this information can be converted into pictures on a computer screen.

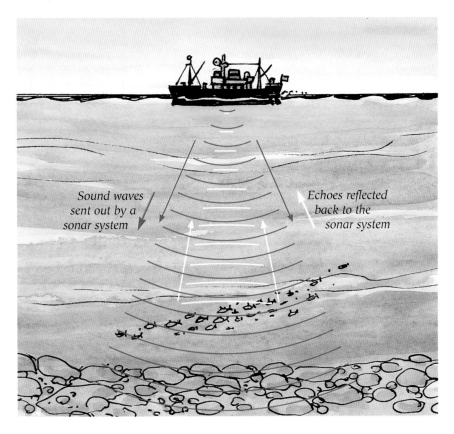

Sound waves sent out by a sonar system

Echoes reflected back to the sonar system

The scientists from Operation Deepscan and Project Urquhart used sonar equipment to investigate the murky waters of the loch. Sonar lets researchers "see" into depths that are too vast and dark for divers to explore.

Sonar boats from Operation Deepscan moved slowly across the water in a straight line, scanning the loch for any signs of life.

Do you think a monster could escape sonar detection?

This sonar tracking grid was constructed by two electronics engineers. It was designed to produce a sonar "picture" of any large object that passed beneath it.

Scientists analyze sonar information on computer screens.

Through sonar investigation, scientists did discover that Loch Ness was much deeper than they had previously thought. They also detected strong sonar signals from a large mysterious object halfway down the loch. These signals lasted for about two minutes, but produced only blurry images on the computer screen. No one knows if the signals were caused by Nessie, a large school of fish, or swirling currents beneath the loch's surface.

Sonar research ship MV Simrad

WHAT DO YOU BELIEVE?

Even with today's modern technology, scientists have been unable to prove that Nessie actually exists – or, for that matter, that she doesn't. Despite many scientific expeditions, eyewitness reports, and photographs, important questions remain unanswered.

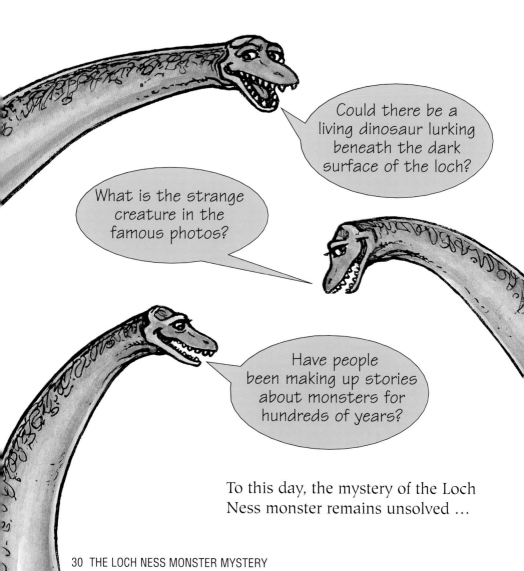

Could there be a living dinosaur lurking beneath the dark surface of the loch?

What is the strange creature in the famous photos?

Have people been making up stories about monsters for hundreds of years?

To this day, the mystery of the Loch Ness monster remains unsolved …

GLOSSARY

castor oil oil made from castor beans used to treat minor illnesses

coelacanth a prehistoric fish that lived millions of years ago

extinct the word used to describe a species of plant or animal that no longer exists on the Earth

glacier a slow-moving river of ice. Glaciers are powerful enough to carve valleys out of mountains.

Ice Age a time in the Earth's history when a layer of ice covered large areas of the planet

landlocked surrounded on all sides by land

peat rotting plant material

plesiosaurs the name for a group of prehistoric sea creatures that lived between 65 and 220 million years ago

prehistoric before recorded time

shoal the name for a group or "school" of fish

sonar a way of detecting objects under the water. Sound waves are sent out and reflected by objects in their path, producing echoes that form a picture on a computer screen.

sound waves the movement of air or water caused by a vibrating object. Sound waves travel in all directions from their source.

INDEX

TITLES IN THE SERIES

The Australian Picture Library: (Urquhart Castle, page 3). *The Image Bank: Jake Rajs* (Loch Ness, pages 4-5). *Fortean Picture Library: Jennifer Bruce* (Loch Ness monster, pages 16-17); *M. P. Meaney* (monster net, page 24); *Ivor Newby* (remote-controlled submarine, page 26); Project Urquhart (researchers aboard MV Simrad, page 26; scientists, MV Simrad, page 29); *Anthony Shiels* (Loch Ness monster, cover, page 9); *R. K. Wilson* (Loch Ness monster, page 8); *Nicholas Witchell* (Operation Deepscan sonar boats, sonar tracking grid, page 28). *G. R. Roberts:* (glacier, post-glacial valley, page 5).